Building Emotional Strength

Strengthen Your Emotional Intelligence to Improve Social Skills, Relationships, Happiness, and Quality of Life

Healthy Habits

About Healthy Habits

Healthy Habits is a team of researchers and writers who provide people with information which has the potential to improve the quality of their lives.

The Healthy Habits team believes that excellent health is more important than anything else in life.

We cover a wide range of healthy practices that people from all over the world have been utilizing for thousands of years.

We hope that you not only enjoy this book, but you also find at least one piece of information that can improve your overall quality of life.

Table of Contents

About Healthy Habits

Healthy Habits is a team of researchers and writers who provide people with information which has the potential to improve the quality of their lives.

The Healthy Habits team believes that excellent health is more important than anything else in life.

We cover a wide range of healthy practices that people from all over the world have been utilizing for thousands of years.

We hope that you not only enjoy this book, but you also find at least one piece of information that can improve your overall quality of life.

Table of Contents

Defining Intelligence

Intelligence is one of the thorniest human features, since people have tried for ages to identify its exact substance and the way it works. Moreover, those engaged in this evasive task have trouble establishing whether there is actually a connection between the level of intelligence a person has and the life standard they manage to achieve. The intelligence quotient, IQ for short, represents one method psychologists have used to measure people's intellectual abilities.

The British psychologist Graham Jones is one of those who believes that general success in life relies on a high IQ. However, he also discovered, by talking to a lot of subjects working in leadership positions in various domains, that having the skills and knowing how to use them right are two sides of the same coin.

At the beginning of this century, Robert Sternberg, professor of human development at Cornell University, elaborated a theory known as "successful intelligence", which shifts the previous simplifying view on intelligence seen as consisting of a series of general abilities subordinated to a main, more developed one. It introduced a complex perspective that allows the personal element to take control.

The warrant of a successful life is the personal ability to use one's strengths at maximum potential and improve one's weaknesses which could otherwise lead to failure. A successfully intelligent person will establish significant goals and set off to achieve them relying, at the same time, on the cultural context they emerged from and keep their ways within the boundaries of honest ethics.

Success in life is strongly related to emotional intelligence (abbreviated EI) which can be defined as the ability to manage your own emotions and the emotions of others. The higher EI a person succeeds to generate, the greater the quality of life they will gain on the long term. EI is crucial in building and preserving healthy relationships, and it also helps a person handle powerful emotions, such as anger, which can get in the way of proper communication.

Defining Leadership

When it comes to defining leadership, psychologists who specialize in the business world know how important it is for leaders to increase their EI. It is a growing trend in modern society to improve one's leading abilities via enhancing emotional intelligence. EI is useful when negotiating a contract or when having to deal with employees and business partners. EI teaches leaders about themselves, allowing them to better understand what sort of feeling shifts they undergo and the reasons behind those shifts.

The concept of transformational leadership was introduced in 1978 by James MacGregor Burns, a pioneer in the field of leadership, and it tells about the leader's ability to become an inspiration, a model for those who chose to follow them. Transformative leaders believe in innovation, encourage creativity, and support their workers in their efforts to achieve ambitious goals. Their charisma attracts and inspires the people around them, who want to do their best to be part of their leader's vision. The fascination of change, the transforming energy emanated by a good leader, an ideal boss, makes workers strive to reach a common destination, to fulfil a dream that has subtly become theirs too.

The qualities of a great leader are not required only in company leading positions. It is valuable for anyone to be an emotionally intelligent leader in everyday life situations as well as in one's family and love relationships. They can learn how to regulate their emotions by noticing simple observations like what triggers a particular sort of reaction, and then firmly deciding not to act under its command. It is always a good idea for someone who is feeling rage to settle in and stop to consider its grounds before doing anything they will probably regret later.

The level of EI one is born with doesn't have to stay the same, fortunately. Nowadays people have the opportunity to heighten their emotional intelligence.

Success in Career Based on High EI

Since 2004, studies about the connection between academic performance and job efficiency have been compared to emotional intelligence and job efficiency. The results from these studies have helped employers to hire people qualified in identifying the EI level of candidates in their human resources departments. It has been established by many companies that a low IQ in employees is partly compensated by high EI.

Other studies advocate that EI's impact on managerial work demands are not always positive, as teamwork productivity drops related to the job context. A gender difference might be the reason, since women generally have higher EI than men. In various circumstances, people with high EI performed equally well compared to their peers who scored lower in EI measuring tests.

Overall, studies agree that emotional intelligence plays a more important role in attaining career success than IQ. People with strong EI find it easier to cope with tasks because their self confidence is high. They also have a better understanding of their own feelings and do not give in to emotional pressure. This allows them to perform effectively even in stressful circumstances.

Research focusing on work relationships found that employees with high EI manage to invest more time and interest in bonding with their supervisors. This could of course influence performance evaluation results. Psychologists who specialize in the field of EI have looked for various ways of measuring it's presence and found three main methods: one based on abilities, the second on self-reported abilities, and the last one using mixed models, such as questionnaires or GENOS.

In spite of these serious attempts at founding a scientific approach to EI measuring and identifying its overall impact on job performance, some researchers object that the reputation of such studies were increased by the media and their importance is not really that great.

However, when facing the burnout syndrome, also known as emotional exhaustion, those employees who possess high doses of optimism and better social skills (two important components of emotional intelligence) find it easier to perform their duties.

Anxiety and Emotional Regulation

A recent study, whose results were published in the journal Emotion, conducted by psychologists at the University of Illinois, studied people who choose to reevaluate a situation which put some emotional pressure on them. The study found that the people who had the ability to shift their perspective from negative to positive tend to experience less anxiety than those who try to restrain their original feelings. The key is to reassess an event by searching for its favorable parts, attempting to dig out something which seems to be disastrous and viewing it as something that looks closer to an opportunity in disguise.

The journal Psychological Science has recently published articles which establish a connection between psychological positivity and good physical health. One of the authors of such studies, Barbara Fredrickson,

Distinguished Professor of Psychology and principal investigator of the Positive Emotions and Psychophysiology Laboratory (a.k.a. PEP Lab) at the University of North Carolina at Chapel Hill, observes that people sometimes consider their feelings as uncontrollable as the weather. However, some factors are completely out of reach for a human being, as they are determined by external circumstances. She states that, on the contrary, choosing to react emotionally one way or another is totally under human control.

Emotional balance is helped by meditation techniques such as mindfulness. People who behave with increased awareness and live in the present have less encounters with anxiety, do not change moods so easily, and get all the advantages of high-quality sleep.

Taking control over one's feelings is not impossible. It is strongly connected to thought patterns which should be switched in order to gain three important qualities: flexibility, accuracy and depth. After a person manages to train their thinking process to follow a certain path, they will also develop the ability to manage their feelings too.

This will certainly develop their well-being and diminish stress.

How to Build Emotional Strength

Emotional stability is something people would like to possess so that they do not feel troubled by any wave that rises or lowers their feelings. It is like sailing across an ocean of emotions. It would be preferable for the water to stay still or just ripple around a bit and let one drive its boat confidently and steadily.

The lack of balance when dealing with emotions has only negative consequences on the reactions of the person involved and it generally ruins relationships via miscommunication. Fortunately, emotions can be controlled and tamed with a lot of practice and patience and the results are certainly worthwhile.

When a person feels that they are subject to an attack by another, they simply get defensive and shut down their understanding and tolerance windows. This issue has a simple solution named change of perspective. The so called "attack" can be seen as an attempt to connect. People can learn to relate better with each other, it's all about reaching out.

Because people are so different, their methods when approaching others also varies a lot from individual to individual. And so do their reactions to this approach. With so many variables it seems like a person cannot be in control any longer, which is false. It is only up to each human being to allow any emotional bustle to install itself. They can also decide not to.

Awareness is key. Becoming aware requires some self-inquiry. Are emotions some external entities equipped with the capacity to control the human mind? Are they some sort of crazy programs working on their own without the person's command? No, but they could become so if left to themselves. The human being is the master of his inner emotional waters. They obey him, once he is able to think his way out of overwhelming feelings. The balanced individual is in control of his/her emotions and takes no action on impulse, staying aware and assessing the circumstances.

People should be able to preserve their sensibility whenever they receive a remark from another person. What they tend to do instead is interpret it for the worst, get emotional about it, feel offended and maybe even fight back using a harsh reply that leaves little room for a positive meaning. From this point on, the conflict can escalate if a person does not decide to behave wisely and put an end to it. Let us think of a common illustration. A man tells a woman "your hair looks different", she reads it as "your hair looks terrible". Or she could just stop and breathe in deeply before replying, assess this statement as a compliment instead and decide to answer by saying "thanks". She is in charge of dealing with the situation as smoothly as possible, no emotional turmoil necessary. She stays down to earth, sensible and aware, refusing to enter the damaging game of misinterpretation.

Another thing strong emotionally intelligent people learn to do is communicate with their own feelings, rather than suppress them. When a person consciously chooses to listen to their emotions, they begin to enter deeper layers of their personality by growing in self-knowledge and self-appreciation.

Trying to withhold or cover up one's emotions leads to no good. In the long term, they will surface in some kind of outburst that is very likely to knock down everything and everyone in its way. Ignoring one's feelings doesn't get anyone too far, not repressing them on the other hand teaches people how to cope with them and establish strong, reliable connections with their peers. Positivity is crucial when it comes to preserving one's emotional balance. People who realize that there is no use worrying about trifles manage stress a lot easier, having more of a relaxed attitude when facing adversities.

Taking care of oneself is a necessary practice leading to high EI. A stress-free life is possible for those who wisely choose to love themselves, not to be too harsh with their flaws and give themselves a treat of what they enjoy best every now and then. A massage, meditation, breathing exercises, yoga, dancing, singing, a little bit of a daily dose of what makes a person feel connected to their inner force helps them recover from negativity strikes and avoid emotional confusion. The simplest way out of a tensioned situation is breathing. The moment one takes to breathe before reacting to some challenging factor is crucial for the emotional sanity of that person and for the stability of their relationships.

A very important feature of strong emotionally intelligent personalities is a person's ability to get up after a fall and stand tall while facing life's challenges. They know that they are only human and subject to error, they understand that they are entitled to crying and screaming if they feel like it. They are capable of forgiving their trespassers as well as themselves and that enables them to move forward with renewed energy and confidence.

Factors Hindering Emotional Balance

People who tend to take things personally have a hard time finding their inner peace. They get paranoid because they are not capable of letting others know how they feel, expecting instead those close to them to just guess what their emotions are. Since such presumptions are farfetched even for the persons dearest to them, they start to nurture feelings of frustration, assuming that they are undesirable and unloved. One must accept the simple truth that the way others relate to them is based on the other persons level of EI.

A person cannot and should never be held responsible for how anyone else reacts to them, ignores them or actually shows they care. Everyone has the right to be selfish and not become interested in the way others might be feeling. It is not the action of an external factor that makes a person have certain negative feelings such as frustration and worthlessness, it is their own choice to interpret that outside cause negatively and let its energy flow within, marring qualities in its way, turning light into darkness, shine into shade. Therefore, people who try to put the blame on everyone else, but their own self are in the wrong.

Those who look for emotional strength in their life choose their battles wisely. That means they will not argue uselessly or heed the mean words others throw at them. Insignificant issues, such as rude comments or unreasonable bitterness are considered to be seen as mere trifles. They do understand that other people have their own educational and cultural background, their personal set of misfortunes which are conducive to uttering insults based on a generally bad mood and lack of satisfaction. When others respond with the same tone and approach, they only prove themselves to be as weak as those challenging them, putting their respectability at stake. Emotional intelligence helps people brace themselves in the front of defiance and move out of the

Factors Hindering Emotional Balance

People who tend to take things personally have a hard time finding their inner peace. They get paranoid because they are not capable of letting others know how they feel, expecting instead those close to them to just guess what their emotions are. Since such presumptions are farfetched even for the persons dearest to them, they start to nurture feelings of frustration, assuming that they are undesirable and unloved. One must accept the simple truth that the way others relate to them is based on the other persons level of EI.

A person cannot and should never be held responsible for how anyone else reacts to them, ignores them or actually shows they care. Everyone has the right to be selfish and not become interested in the way others might be feeling. It is not the action of an external factor that makes a person have certain negative feelings such as frustration and worthlessness, it is their own choice to interpret that outside cause negatively and let its energy flow within, marring qualities in its way, turning light into darkness, shine into shade. Therefore, people who try to put the blame on everyone else, but their own self are in the wrong.

Those who look for emotional strength in their life choose their battles wisely. That means they will not argue uselessly or heed the mean words others throw at them. Insignificant issues, such as rude comments or unreasonable bitterness are considered to be seen as mere trifles. They do understand that other people have their own educational and cultural background, their personal set of misfortunes which are conducive to uttering insults based on a generally bad mood and lack of satisfaction. When others respond with the same tone and approach, they only prove themselves to be as weak as those challenging them, putting their respectability at stake. Emotional intelligence helps people brace themselves in the front of defiance and move out of the "battlefield" without entering a dispute, firmly holding onto their dignity and freedom of choice.

A mindful response to a situation is expected from someone who has attained emotional strength rather than a mere simplistic reaction. Their intuition helps such people get over the first emotional burst of frustration or anger and find a reasonable solution by being able to see the whole picture and refusing to put up with the apparently easy way out that a quick reaction offers. It is similar to consciously choosing to take a stroll out there in the heavy rain in order to gain the ability to enjoy the sunshine after the short satisfaction of a shower.

Emotionally balanced people don't give in to despair. They know there is always a bright side of things and circumstances will surely change to their advantage soon enough. They do not perceive danger and terror as final, because hope never dies in strong hearts. Many a time, human beings fail to get perspective on a certain matter and their world seems to be crashing down to pieces all around. Lifting their heads above this vision of disaster, emotionally strong individuals manage to move on, to see the shimmering light waiting for them at the end of a struggle and decide to keep going in spite of all odds. The idea that the world is coming to an end is not part of their plan. Time proves them right over and over again.

Staying present in their momentary emotions helps people build up more strength in this domain. It is crucial that they fall not in the trap of connecting a present failure to a story in the past, as this can create a pattern and any similar situation in the future will follow it. Past negative issues are not healthy for one's EI. A person with a high emotional balance knows to deal with a negative emotion and just take it for what it is, a mere emotion, with no added value. They would not try to hide a feeling of fear or frustration rising from an unsuccessful state since they are most likely aware of the fact that such an attitude could cause more damage. They understand the power available to them in the present moment and act accordingly: neither past concerns summoned, nor future menace hanging at the horizon.

Resisting change is not an option. If it is bound to happen, it will. This doesn't mean determinism is the answer, yet a simple observation of the natural, social, and cultural environment can convince anyone that times are changing. Trying to run away from this truth would not be helpful, moreover it could be prejudicial to one's emotional wellbeing. The earth keeps spinning hour after hour, the ocean sends wave after wave to caress the sand under the spell of the moon, seasons follow one after the other and people grow. How could one refuse growth?

An ancient Latin saying goes like this: "errare humanum est" - "to make mistakes is human." Everyone is subject to error. People disappoint other people and still deserve their love and care. Pretending to be perfect can only lead to a lessening of self-esteem whenever a chance to err comes one's way again. Who are they trying to fool when they claim they are infallible? Do they consider themselves super-human? People with this kind of approach to life risk triggering harsh judgement from others for building up a big empty lie.

It is also clear for advanced EI people that negative self-assessment is not worthwhile. The roots of such a misperception generally come from the personal past when, at some dark point, someone judged a person for a flaw and that person started to nourish self-hatred. A human being doesn't come into this world with such harming feelings towards their own person, nor should they continue to embrace a lie that labels one as worthless. Instead they decide to feel love for themselves by nurturing positive thoughts. It is again a conscious choice meant to bring about changes in the quality of life people lead.

Meditation and Emotional Stability

The regular practice of meditation is strongly recommended for those who are trying hard to enhance their emotional control. Nowadays, people are struggling with anxiety and depression, they shift their mood too easily especially due to the stressful environment they live in. In order to feel calm and composed, to gain peace and quiet in one's life, a person should start meditating right away. The positive effects of this technique are visible immediately, as well as over time. Both the body and mind begin to relax and become less vulnerable to outside pressure. The level of hormones released by stress into the human body gets regulated and then decreases by meditation practice which involves controlled breathing.

Once a person learns the habit of breathing properly and quieting the mind, they will be ready to face new challenges when it comes to everyday stressful situations, such as tensions at the workplace or family issues. The fake image of life as a hazardous jump into the void that is thrilling and scary at the same time can be transformed by meditation into a more realistic and healthier view. It gives one the freedom to choose their own perspective on life. Life generally equates to what one decides to make of it. With a stable attitude anyone would feel prepared to heal wounds from the past, to erect self-esteem like flying a kite of freedom visible from a distance in order to encourage the same approach in others who fear trying new things, introducing unfamiliar practices into their comfort zone, which alas confines them to feel so uncomfortable.

When people start visualizing their future, they actually begin forging it. The power of thinking is real, and meditation can provide a person with the proper tools for making the most out of their present life and also for mapping out great expectations. A change from within emerging in broad daylight - this could be a definition of what meditation is eventually all about.

Emotional Strength and Writing

Traumatic events, a stressful environment, various forms of addiction, anxiety and depression can have diminished effects on people who practice therapeutic writing. A lot of people use writing as a healing tool without even realizing it. Keeping a diary in which one can discharge their concerns and frustrations is a well-known means of coping with the troubling changes teenage years bring along. Many a time, it seems easier for people to communicate their feelings in writing rather than speaking. That happens because writing a letter or an email to another about personal feelings confers certain advantages: one can take their time thinking it over, choosing their words carefully, avoiding an immediate response or being interrupted as it happens in oral communication. Writing is releasing. It has an undeniable cathartic effect which professional writers are perfectly aware of.

It is a well-known fact now, approved by scientists, that writing as therapy really works. This is not just a trendy practice recommended by modern psychologists as it has been used for half a century with indisputable success. Writing is there for us all. One does not have to be especially born for it. Anyone can write about their feelings, confide in the blankness of mute pages which can cope with anything, as Cicero once put it "epistula non erubescit" - "a letter doesn't blush".

People who suffer, certain groups undergoing upsetting experiences, such as prisoners, persons diagnosed with chronic diseases, teenagers or mentally ill individuals are more prone to writing than the rest of us. They feel drawn to this liberating technique as they know it helps them feel better, understand their experience thoroughly, get some perspective, become able to envisage a positive future again, to gain some hope in recovery, in deliverance from a present distressful environment. Writing encourages them to look their feelings in the face and learn to cope with whatever got them there in the first place.

For young people writing proves to be an effective way of expressing their emotions and thus learning how to deal with them in a conscious and controlled manner. This is why creative writing is such a popular course in high schools and colleges. The average teenager can benefit from this precious tool, but moreover children and youth at risk have the opportunity to embrace this practice and release their negativity.

The main risks for at risk people are dropping out of school, drug or/and alcohol use, juvenile delinquency, becoming homeless because they leave home, being abused or exploited, and having mental disorders. The sad fact is that children at risk can rarely be identified beforehand, most of them having already suffered from one of these factors before getting any help from the grown-ups. They would be quiet about their damaging experience due to various reasons. Either trying to protect those they hold dear though systematically hurting them or considering it normal and figuring that all kids go through similar stuff. There is shame and guilt enveloping their dreams and they sometimes manage to emerge back to the surface and safety of emotional stability by being given the chance to write openly about their experience. Organizations aiming to support youth at risk encourage them to write not only journals, but also fictional stories based on their ordeals or maybe poetry and even autobiographical pieces.

Troubled young persons have the opportunity to benefit from the implementation of writing therapy programs in schools, mental institutions, juvenile halls, and some other disadvantaged areas. Sometimes they are asked and guided to create plays which can be performed on stage by themselves or with their colleagues. Thus, kids at risk get involved in other dramas whose characters they may identify with and feel more accepted. This can lead to a realizing that they are not alone in this struggle. Community centers as well as children's clubs welcome writing therapy techniques among the methods that inspire troubled youth to pour out their emotional issues. This is particularly helpful when someone is avoiding face to face talks or individual counselling which can be more challenging. The results of introducing writing practices among teens is remarkable: they tend to score better in school tests, their literacy is polished up, they become more mature emotionally and mentally, their self-esteem has to benefit, they achieve a higher degree of empathy and an improved understanding of the self.

Likewise, writing therapy procedures can be successfully applied in adult cases. As they write about their traumatizing past experiences or describe the feelings connected to their criminal history, troubled grown-ups gradually become able to cope with their mistakes or to forgive the others for the damage brought upon their lives. Writing about one's personal trials is definitely a healthy way of getting out of trouble and staying on the safe side both for children and adults and it also helps those who haven't been in a similar situation become more empathic.

Downsides of Emotional Strength

All the advantages of cultivating emotional intelligence mentioned above are undoubtedly genuine. That is why, EI is studied in secondary schools, medical and business educational institutes. The bigger the credit given to this subject, the less open people are to admitting it. This phenomenon also presents certain risks. For instance, it is easy for powerful people who learn to control their emotions and those of others to manipulate and persuade individuals and even crowds to act in a certain way, contrary to their best interest.

One famous example of such a public figure who practiced modeling body language to be emotionally convincing is Adolf Hitler. Studies and photographs dedicated to his life prove that he was not a natural born manipulator, but a self-taught one. He asked Heinrich Hoffmann, who was a professional photographer, to keep to face talks or individual counselling which can be more challenging. The results of introducing writing practices among teens is remarkable: they tend to score better in school tests, their literacy is polished up, they become more mature emotionally and mentally, their self-esteem has to benefit, they achieve a higher degree of empathy and an improved understanding of the self.

Likewise, writing therapy procedures can be successfully applied in adult cases. As they write about their traumatizing past experiences or describe the feelings connected to their criminal history, troubled grown-ups gradually become able to cope with their mistakes or to forgive the others for the damage brought upon their lives. Writing about one's personal trials is definitely a healthy way of getting out of trouble and staying on the safe side both for children and adults and it also helps those who haven't been in a similar situation become more empathic.

Downsides of Emotional Strength

All the advantages of cultivating emotional intelligence mentioned above are undoubtedly genuine. That is why, EI is studied in secondary schools, medical and business educational institutes. The bigger the credit given to this subject, the less open people are to admitting it. This phenomenon also presents certain risks. For instance, it is easy for powerful people who learn to control their emotions and those of others to manipulate and persuade individuals and even crowds to act in a certain way, contrary to their best interest.

One famous example of such a public figure who practiced modeling body language to be emotionally convincing is Adolf Hitler. Studies and photographs dedicated to his life prove that he was not a natural born manipulator, but a self-taught one. He asked Heinrich Hoffmann, who was a professional photographer, to keep a record of the images in which he rehearsed specific postures and gestures meant to trigger certain emotions in the audience. Then he would look back at them and decide whether or not it was a good option to introduce those poses in his speeches. He was a very modern politician who knew exactly how to take advantage of the people's need to feel part of an emotionally connected community, united by a common goal, however cruel and unbelievably inhuman that may have been.

A study co-authored by Jochen Menges, University Lecturer in Organizational Behavior at Cambridge Business School, shows that over-charismatic leaders compel their followers to suppress their emotions and behave as if enchanted, without being capable of critical thinking and reasoning. This awestruck effect leaves the people listening to an inspiring speech unable to remember much of its content, although they are under the impression that they can recall a lot of information. Since the focus of the speech falls not on the message but on the feelings transmitted by the presenter, the audience is so moved that they behave as dumbstruck. These mesmerizing consequences are not healthy for the leader's followers, as they are left to deal with too much emotional charge they cannot release.

Employees with high EI can easily learn how to manipulate their peers in their personal interest. Stéphane Côté, professor of organizational behavior at the Rotman School of Management at the University of Toronto, led a study on the relationship between the emotional quotient and the Machiavellian tendencies in employees. The results clearly show that people who are inclined to see others as mere means to an end use their emotional intelligence to mask their true feelings and undermine their colleagues.

University College London professor Martin Kilduff led a team of researchers who studied the recently discovered dark side of EI. People with high emotional intelligence can also learn to fake certain emotions expected from them in order to get some advantages at the workplace and are willing to climb on others just to get at the top.

Conclusion

In 1990, psychologists Peter Salovey at Yale and John Mayer at the University of New Hampshire created the concept of EI. Five years later, Daniel Goleman made the idea famous in his book entitled Emotional Intelligence. Since then, the evolution of research in this field was hindered by unscientific measurements, such as the unreliable self-report method. People asked to assess their own emotional skills are always subjective when stating things like: "I am good at understanding other people's feelings". As a matter of fact, this part of psychology specializing in the study and measurement of EI, which definitely has plenty of uses in various fields of human activity, is still under construction.

Emotional balance is an important asset which people should try to gain and preserve, since it enhances the quality of life in so many domains. Stable feelings, such as calm, peace of mind and understanding prepare one's soul for staying connected to the whole of existence.

People also need to understand that emotional intelligence can become a tool for negativity in the wrong hands. There will always be those who try to take advantage of others and manipulate them because the former category only follows personal goals and haven't got higher moral values.

Thanks for Reading

Thank you for investing in your health.

It is an honor to know that our readers are gaining a massive amount of value from our books. It is very much appreciated when a reader leaves a review which explain what they liked most about the book.

We also appreciate advice on any improvements that you would like to see. In addition to this, please feel free to let us know if there are any topics that you would like us to write about.